W9-ARP-140

In praise of *Who Moved My Church?*

"This positively provocative portrayal of the twenty-first century church is definitely worth the read. Be very careful because if you dare read *Who Moved My Church?*, get ready to be moved as well as inspired."

Walt Kallestad
Senior Pastor, Community of Joy
Phoenix, Arizona

"*Who Moved My Church?* is a delightful allegory on the way we do church in the twenty-first century. It strikes boldly at our customs, traditions and church operations. Anyone reading this book will be challenged to rethink every aspect of church ministry. Be prepared to change!"

Stan Toler
Author and Pastor
Oklahoma City, Oklahoma

"Mike Nappa is a storyteller for our times. He writes with humor that is to the point and a grace that brings hope for the 'churchified.' Read this book at the risk of causing positive change in your life and church."

Andy Freeman
Executive Producer, The 700 Club

"This little book packs a big punch. Mike Nappa gets you thinking, smiling, and asking yourself, 'Is my church focused on God's priorities or on man's distractions?' The answers will not only help readers become more effective members of the body of Christ, but also help church staff and lay leaders achieve their full potential in ministry."

Dan Benson
Author, 12 Stupid Things People Do with Their Money

"Get ready to have your buttons pushed! *Who Moved My Church?* will open your eyes to some attitudes within the American church that need to be examined, and at the same time it will move you deeply. It's a quick read, and it'll take you on a path that every believer should walk—an honest evaluation of your own heart. Mike Nappa hits the mark."

Clay Jacobsen
Television Producer and Novelist

"Reading *Who Moved My Church?* may endanger your comfort level! Mike Nappa's parable challenged me to look at my own attitudes and lifestyle—but Mike also left me with a sense of excitement about how we can share the good news of Jesus Christ with our world in a powerful, relevant way."

Dr. Norm Wakefield
Professor of Pastoral Ministry at Phoenix Seminary

"Mike Nappa's take on the sometimes factious voices within the church is humorous, insightful, and extremely timely. It'll change how you look at Christian history and current events."

Jefferson Scott,
Novelist/Author of Christian technothriller
Fatal Defect

"A parable packed with wit and wonder. Mike Nappa imagines a church that Jesus Christ would be proud to call His own. Read this book and your own church will never be the same."

Dr. Diane Komp
Author, Why Me? A Doctor Examines the Book of Job

"The characters of *Who Moved My Church?* look all too familiar—I see myself in them. With humor, tact, and the stroke of a pen, Mike Nappa presents a gentle—yet urgent—challenge for all of us who claim the name of Christ today. Read this book. We all need to."

Mike Jones
Executive Director, Reach Ministries International

"In the best tradition of parables, such as *Pilgrim's Progress, Who Moved My Church?* is a thought-provoking story that provides log-plucking activity for anyone who reads it, and heart-softening material for all who are willing to listen and apply. Read it and consider if your own life, like JC Cathedral, is under construction, being built into something healthy and new."

Sandra Byrd
Best-selling Novelist

"*Who Moved My Church?* seeks to get us thinking about where the church is and where it ought to be."

John Duckworth
Author, Stories That Sneak Up On You

"The amusing story contained in this little book may well ruffle your feathers. But it'll open your eyes to what's happening to our churches—and to what your church can become."

Thom and Joani Schultz
Authors, Why Nobody Learns Much of Anything at Church: And How to Fix It

Who Moved My Church?

Who Moved My Church?

A Story About Discovering Purpose in a Changing Culture

by
Mike Nappa

Tulsa, Oklahoma

Unless otherwise indicted, all Scripture quotations are taken from the King James Version of the Bible.

Scripture quotations marked NIV are taken from the Holy Bible, New International Version®. NIV®. Copyright © 1973, 1978, 1984 by International Bible Society. Used by permission of Zondervan Publishing House. All rights reserved.

Who Moved My Church?
A Story About Discovering Purpose in a Changing Culture
ISBN 1-58919-990-1

Published by RiverOak Publishing
P.O. Box 700143
Tulsa, OK 74170-0143

The characters and events in this book are fictional, and any resemblance to actual persons or events is coincidental.

For Kent Hummel and Tom Davis,
who keep our church moving.

Contents

Foreword

I have been teaching the principles of leadership—of becoming a person of influence—for what feels like my entire life!

Influence may always begin with the individual, but it doesn't stop there. Companies, organizations, associations, and, yes, churches exert tremendous leadership in their communities and the world.

We live in a rapidly changing, and, at times, highly volatile, culture. Jesus reminded His disciples that they would indeed always live in the world, but challenged them not to be just like the world (John 17:15,16). St. Paul picked up the same theme when he reminded the church not to be conformed by the world, but to be transformed on the inside through total commitment to God (Romans 12:2).

Mike Nappa has written an intelligent, clever, and *explosive* book that challenges the people of God to consider what kind of influence they will exercise in the world today.

Who Moved My Church? will entertain you. You will laugh, cry, probably get mad, and, most importantly, think.

So if you feel that someone has moved your church, read this book—and then get out there and find it!

John C. Maxwell
Founder, The INJOY Group

"He did not say anything to them without using a parable. . . ."

—Mark 4:34 NIV

A Workshop in Denver

The workshop leader opened the door and was relieved to see that there were people waiting to come in. Too often at big conventions like this one in Denver, the majority of attendees overlooked these little "sidelight" seminars, flocking instead to hear the "big name" speakers—and he definitely wasn't famous. The leader smiled and greeted folks as they drifted into the room to take their seats.

On the whiteboard at the front of the room he had written the title of his seminar: "Christianity & Culture: Where Do We Fit In?" *I probably should have come up with a more exciting title,* he thought. He now moved up near the podium and stole furtive glances to see if he could discover anything about the people who were coming in.

Two well-dressed women came through the doorway chatting and took seats right up front. One wore classy jewelry and a perfect smile that made her look much like a famous gospel diva. The other wore long, straight hair and a conservative business suit.

A younger man—college age, maybe?—sat a few rows behind them, and, seeing that he was early, quickly flipped open a notebook and began sketching people he saw in the room. Two chairs to his left, another woman slipped into a seat. Leaning over, she silently opened a Bible and, cupping her hands around her face as if to block out distractions, studied a passage of Scripture intently as if memorizing it. And in the back, three loud men came laughing into the small assembly, clapping each other on the back and reminiscing about a recent golf game.

There were others too, but the seminar leader didn't have time to study everyone. It was time to begin.

Stepping to the podium, the leader

cleared his throat and smiled. "Welcome," he said. "I hope you all came to the right place. This is the workshop on Christianity and culture."

Loud Man #1 feigned a shocked look and pretended to dart for the door, eliciting chuckles from his cohorts and a few others in the room. The leader smiled again, "Right! Last chance to get out," he laughed. Then, after giving everyone a moment to settle in, the leader spoke again.

"Well, I'm glad you've all come, and I hope you're enjoying your time at this convention so far. Let's start off with a question: Why are you here? Or, in other words, what made you want to come to this particular seminar?"

There was a moment of silence, then Gospel Diva spoke up. "I have a friend, and she keeps telling me that Christians are all either irrelevant or boring. Sometimes I'm afraid I have to agree with her. So I'm here to find out why that's so in our society."

Sketcher put down his pencil and pushed aside his sketchbook. "I think," he said, "that I don't know what to think." He paused, trying to collect his thoughts. "I mean, there are so many messages that bombard all of us every day—read this book, don't watch this movie, boycott this TV show, and stuff—that I often find myself confused about what I should and shouldn't be doing as a Christian."

Bible Memory Girl nodded, adding, "Yeah, me too. I hate to say it, but sometimes that old 'What Would Jesus Do?' slogan just isn't enough for me because I honestly *don't know* what Jesus would do in my situations."

Loud Man #3 spoke, in a voice that was quieter than Leader expected. He said, "You know, if I read my Bible correctly, it seems to me that when Jesus was on this earth He somehow managed to be totally immersed in His Jewish culture without becoming stained by the sin in that culture." He shrugged. "That's what I'd like to learn how to do, so that's why I'm here."

The leader nodded and looked thoughtful. Loud Man #1, grinning, spoke up again, "So there you have it, Teach," he said. "What have you got for us, then? Six Steps to Cultural Relevance? Five Principles for Holy Living in an Unholy World? Seven Spiritual Slogans for Every Section of Life?"

"Actually," said the leader, "I don't have any pat answers or sermon outlines for you today. Just a lot of questions like the ones you've already asked. That and a story that someone told me recently. I'd like to tell it to you now. It's not a long story. It's called 'Who Moved My Church?' I think maybe it can help us all think through what it means to be Christians in our culture today."

And so he began.

Act One: The Occurrence in Municipa City

Scene One: *The Reporter's Arrival*

The Reporter shifted his weight uncomfortably. It was a strange assignment really. Spend the next several years watching groups of humans respond to an action by the Publisher. The Reporter stretched his frame almost instinctively. He wasn't even there yet, and he already felt the claustrophobic stress of that place.

Still, it was an assignment that was very important to the Publisher. And one the Reporter intended to do well. He flipped open the project pad and reread the instructions:

1. Enter Earth's atmosphere.
2. Observe the actions and reactions of the people associated with JC Cathedral in Municipa City, USA.
3. Chronicle the progress of the church members.
4. Note the practices and principles in play during the observation period.
5. Remain on assignment until the Publisher calls for your report.

The Reporter sighed. It certainly didn't seem like a plum assignment for a worker with his experience. But, he reasoned, that didn't really matter. What mattered was what the Publisher wanted, and that was enough reason for the Reporter to do his very best.

With a calm urgency, he first carefully folded his wings behind him until they were invisible to the naked eye. "Might as well look the part," he whispered to himself. By the time he landed on the ground he was wearing lightweight wool slacks and a button-down dress shirt, with a loosened tie dangling from an opened collar. In one hand he held a microcassette recorder, in the other a notepad and pen. Around his neck was a slightly battered—but high quality—rangefinder camera.

The Reporter paused to take in his appearance. It wasn't necessary, really. The citizens of Municipa City couldn't see him unless the Reporter allowed it. But to dress like this made him *feel* more like the role he was to play—and for the first time, it felt good.

The Reporter stood on the lawn across the street from the JC Cathedral. The church was just on the outskirts of town, a short drive from the nicest section of the city. He button his shirt collar, straightened the tie and opened his notepad.

The sun was just beginning to peek over the horizon when the Reporter clicked on his tape recorder. He gazed across the street and spoke, "Municipa City, day one."

Then he took in the sunrise and waited, which was just fine with him. Waiting was something he did very well.

Scene Two:
The Shocking Discovery

Althea Spire saw it—or rather, didn't see it—first. She was usually more than two hours early for the church service. In fact, she often got there early enough to witness the breathtaking last moments of a beautiful sunrise. She liked to come early, liked the silence of the big old church close to dawn. She even had her own key to the building, and often she would come on Sundays before it opened, let herself in, and spend an hour or so in the little prayer chapel southeast of the main sanctuary. This made her more tolerant when the masses arrived—the noisy, sloppily dressed, disrespectful hordes who came to this place of peace and turned it into a din of activity.

She frowned at that thought, then smiled. *Something should be done,* she said to herself, just as she did each Sunday at this time. It was her first smile of the day. For some inexplicable reason, her alarm clock had failed to sound this morning. She had checked it three different times, as was her custom, but still it had remained silent. Thus, for the first time in who knows how long, Spire did not arrive with the sunrise. And even though the service would not begin for another fifteen minutes, Spire felt late. And, consequently, nothing felt right.

But even Spire did not expect this.

She stared at the sign on the corner. "JC Cathedral" it said proudly. Yes, this was definitely the right place. And yet something was wrong. Terribly wrong.

Spire was still standing and staring when Randall Cuff arrived. Neither one said a word to the other, though Cuff did emit a mild profanity under his breath (asking forgiveness from God immediately afterward, of course). Spire looked at him out of the corner of her eyes, not totally surprised at what he said. She would talk to Cuff about his language later. Now they had a *real* problem.

Moments later, Eliara Link arrived—just before the service was to start, as usual—and stood next to them, oblivious to the silence of the situation.

"What in heaven's name happened

here?" she fairly shouted. "Randall? Althea? What's going on?"

Spire simply grimaced, and Cuff just cleared his throat, as if he were going to say something, and then changed his mind. Finally, Nameless came on the scene, eating a freshly bought doughnut and carrying a paper cup filled with coffee.

"Nameless!" loudmouthed Link, "it's about time you got here." She motioned toward the church property and demanded, "Have you an explanation for *that?*"

Nameless choked on a bite of doughnut and spilled coffee on his shirt, which in turn made him hop around in disgust and pain.

There was a brief moment of silence. Then, as if all four had finally taken in the enormity of the situation at the same time, Spire, Cuff, Link, and Nameless all said to each other:

"Who moved my church?!"

True, the JC Cathedral sign still stood on the corner, and the parking lot still boasted its hundreds of yellow-marked spaces. But where once had been a building filled with all kinds of churchy stuff, there was now only an empty lot.

"It's almost as if God Himself reached down, picked up the building, and transported it away overnight," Nameless said quietly, with awe.

"Oh, for Pete's sake, what kind of crazy mumbo jumbo is that?" grumbled Cuff. "This is obviously the work of vandals. Those Henderson kids—doesn't their dad own that house-moving business?"

"I don't know, Randall," said Link, "seems like somebody would have noticed if a couple of kids were moving *an entire church building.*"

Spire grimaced again. Noise, everywhere noise. *Lord,* she prayed silently, *give me patience—and I want it now!*

It wasn't long before more members of JC Cathedral arrived on the scene. Soon the whole area was filled with people milling around, some praying, some shouting, some calling the police on their cell phones.

"Not a trace of it left," said some.

"It's got to be around here somewhere," said others.

"Maybe we're having a mass hallucination or something."

"What if the city demolished it while we were gone?"

"I'm going to write to my congressman."

"I am your congressman, and I have no idea . . ."

"Search for clues, everybody."

"Where's the pastor?"

"Our God in heaven, we beseech Thee . . ."

"What about church? Are we going to have a church service this morning or not? 'Cause if we're not, I'm outta here."

"Everyone just be quiet!"

Scene Three: *The Searching Starts*

It is amazing how quickly silence can come over a crowd when one person carries a bullhorn. Especially when that person is Randall Cuff, retired army major and current ROTC instructor at the local high school.

A man accustomed to being in charge, Cuff stood patiently in the middle of the crowd. He was very comfortable with the image his personality projected. And if the good soldier's demeanor wasn't enough, there was always his menacing size. Standing just over 6 feet, 4 inches tall, and still blessed with the bulk that had won him a college football scholarship, Cuff was obviously a man people looked up to.

"All right, people," he said when he had everyone's attention, "a church building certainly can't go very far—at least not in this town. I say we organize search parties and get to the bottom of this once and for all. Now listen up!"

Several in the crowd shouted, "Here, here!" and "That's the thing" and "Let's go then." A few others just shrugged their shoulders and started edging quietly away, figuring others would handle the dirty work, and they could take the day off and relax—or maybe catch up on yard work neglected the day before.

In the end, Cuff bellowed and gestured until four groups were formed, with twenty-five "volunteers" in each group. Group One was to be led by Althea Spire, since she was the one most familiar with the interior of the church—except for the pastor, of course. (And where was that pastor anyway? Shouldn't he have been here by now? Althea would speak with him about his absence later. Right now, she needed to care for the needs of her team.)

Randall Cuff took command of Group Two. Eliara Link couldn't bear the thought that Cuff would do something she wouldn't do, so she quickly volunteered to lead Group Three. Cuff rolled his eyes and snorted, but in the end gave a reserved nod of approval for Link.

There was no one to lead Group Four until somebody finally nominated Nameless, and Nameless reluctantly accepted the nomination.

It was decided that the four groups would explore four different sections of the city until one of them found the church, at which point they would send a representative out to tell the other groups where it was.

After a lengthy prayer led by Spire (a few of the volunteers slipped away while most everyone's eyes were closed), the four search teams started out on their journeys.

The Reporter watched the proceedings with a keen eye, and as the crowd was breaking up he drew a sketch on his pad. It was the outline of a church building, and inside the outline he wrote these words:

"When the church is missing, you'd better go out and find it."

Then, catching up with Group One, he fell in line behind Althea, following her on the road toward downtown.

Act Two:
Althea Spire Recalls Nehemiah

Scene One:
"Go to Sixth and Mason"

To be honest, Althea Spire was almost excited about this new little adventure. Sure, she was curious about what had happened to the church and all, but about halfway through the confusion she had hit upon what she thought was the solution to the mystery.

I wonder how he did it, she almost murmured aloud. *Pastor Chase doesn't seem to have that kind of cleverness within him.* She furrowed her brow. Spire wasn't Chase's biggest fan—why wouldn't he wear a coat and tie to Sunday night services? But still, he had somehow managed to move the church overnight and, in doing so, to weed out all those noisy, unkempt, disrespectful people who insisted on coming into God's sanctuary each week.

Once she had figured that out, she knew what she had to do. She carefully assembled the people on her team, choosing only those who—like her—had a deep appreciation for the things of God. Now all she had to do was lead this peaceful little flock to the pastor's hiding place, where she was certain they could create a whole new, respectable church for God.

Althea felt light-headed as she dreamed of the possibilities. It was almost as if God had given the JC Cathedral a second chance at things. A chance to start over, to make things right. To make a church God would be proud of.

"Um, Ms. Spire?" The young lady tapped her shoulder lightly, obviously out of breath. "Um, do you think . . . we could . . . slow down a bit? We seem to have lost Dr. Galler, Mrs. Baker, and several of the others a few blocks back."

Spire looked at the girl's ankle-length skirt approvingly, smiled serenely, and stopped in her tracks. "Of course, dear. Of course." She inhaled deeply. Today was certainly a good day.

When everyone had finally caught up, Spire quietly addressed her followers. "Well," she said warmly, "this is a bit of an adventure. Does anyone have any suggestions as to where we should look first?"

One of the faithful spoke up, "While we were resting back there, we heard two children chattering about the 'new thing' downtown. Maybe we should start there?"

Spire frowned ever so slightly. "Were these children from our church?" she asked.

"Well, no, but—"

"Since when do we take direction from children of the world?"

"Aah, well, good point. I'm sorry. It was just an idea."

Spire surveyed the rest of her group. "Any other suggestions?"

This time no one spoke, so Spire continued, "Then I guess we'd better do what we should've done all along. Let us pray."

"But, Ms. Spire, don't you remember? We just prayed about fifteen minutes ago at the church—well, at the empty lot where the church used to be. Actually, you led the prayer and . . ."

But it was too late. Spire had already motioned for all heads to bow and eyes to close. She cut right in, praying, "Our dear heavenly Father, what a trial we are in today. As You know, someone has moved our church, and we are determined to find it for Your sake, Lord. Lead us, guide us, direct us, show us, steer us, conduct us, channel us, point us, funnel us to Thy path. Into Thy hands we commend our spirits. Amen."

"Ms. Spire," a voice from the back spoke up. "While we were praying, I felt God leading me to a passage of Scripture. I—"

Suddenly three teenagers raced past on skateboards. "Hey, you guys!" they shouted as they passed. "Something just appeared downtown at Sixth and Mason! You gotta go check it out!"

Insolent youths, Spire said to herself. *How dare they interfere with my prayer and Scripture time!* Aloud she only said, "Ignore the interruption, Brother Miles. You were saying?"

"Well, I distinctly felt impressed with the Bible reference 2 Samuel 19:4."

A car whizzed down the street, honking as its occupants shouted, "Sixth and Mason! A miracle has happened at Sixth and Mason!" Soon two more cars and a pickup truck sped that way as well.

Spire tried to block out the activity in the street and focus on the task at hand. *The devil always sends distractions,* she thought.

"Excellent," she said to Brother Miles. She quickly produced a weathered Bible and flipped to the correct passage. "Yes, yes. Let's see, chapter 19, verse 4 says this: 'But the king covered his face, and the king cried with a loud voice, O my son Absalom, O Absalom, my son, my son!'"

"What does it mean, Ms. Spire?"

A knowing look came over Spire's face. She nodded to herself, then to her flock. By now there was a traffic bottleneck out in the road, and dozens of people were cascading through the streets headed toward downtown.

"Obviously," said Spire, "God is telling us how sorrowful He is that His children have rebelled against Him as Absalom did against King David."

Several nodded, but all still looked confused. "Does it mean anything else, Ms. Spire?"

Four more children raced past the party shouting, "Miracle at Sixth and Mason! Miracle at Sixth and Mason!"

Spire sighed. "I believe it means also that perhaps we should move toward downtown." With that she turned and led the way toward Sixth and Mason, if only to make the devil shut up for just a while.

Scene Two:
A Time To Build Walls

When the group arrived at Sixth and Mason, a crowd was already gathered around the spot, buzzing nervously and trying to make sense out of what was there. Spire and her troupe worked through the mass of humanity until they saw it too.

The JC Cathedral. Right there, smack in the middle of downtown Municipa City. Something was different, though. The roof was there, and the steeple. But there were no walls.

"How could they do this to such a sacred place?" Spire whispered in dismay. The building and all its bulwarks were still in place, but the outside walls had been removed as if by magic. The sanctuary was visible from the street, as was the prayer chapel and even the church restrooms!

Most of the people all hung back from this miracle, as some had suggested it was a bomb primed to go off at any moment. A few of the braver ones had ventured inside to give it a look. Spire noted with disdain that they were tracking mud all over the freshly cleaned carpets.

That was too much for Spire. With a wave of her hand she marched her flock straight in where the doors should have been to reclaim that sanctuary for God. "Out, out, out!" she screeched. "This is

God's house! How dare you sully it up like this! OUT!"

Just then the police arrived and, upon hearing Spire's outrage, assumed she was the owner of the property.

"Officer," Spire said as she collared a young policewoman who entered the building. "This is *my* church, and I will not allow it to be defaced and disrespected by all these unholy people pawing through it. Now, are you going to do your job and clear out this temple, or do I have to?"

The police officer looked baffled at first, then nodded curtly and went back to her partner. After a whispered conference, the two of them moved back in and began commanding loiterers to "move along."

"Show's over, time to leave this place in peace," they said to the people. In short time they had dispersed the crowd and left Spire and her people standing on the carpet just outside the sanctuary and staring at the street.

"Look at that," said one of Spire's volunteers with a cluck. "There's a bar right across the street."

"And that theater showing godless movies just to the west of us."

"And that raucous arena to the right."

"Whoever picked this place for our church must have made a mistake," Spire said, shaking her head. "To be placed right in the center of a den of iniquity." Then a gleam formed in her eyes.

"Well, we shall fix that, won't we? Ladies and gentlemen, just as Nehemiah built a wall around Jerusalem, we too shall rebuild the walls of this fine church."

Spire's flock gave a cheer, and they all set to work.

The Reporter watched with interest the reaction of Spire's people to the situation. They didn't know that the Publisher Himself had picked this very spot to place

His new branch office. The Reporter shook his head with confusion and wrote a question on his notepad:

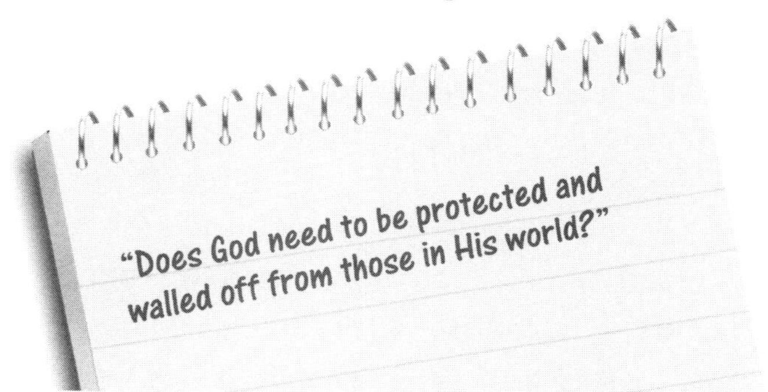

It was a question he would have to deal with later, though. For now, it was time to observe.

Scene Three:
Family Life

It took only three weeks—and much labor and sweat and financial support—for Spire's troupe to build a cloister-type wall around the perimeter of the church. During that time, Spire conveniently put off sending out a messenger to the other groups looking for the JC Cathedral until finally she—and her followers—had quite forgotten all about it.

When they were all safely sealed inside, they hooked up a computer and made arrangements through the Internet for food and supplies to be delivered on a regular basis. Then they devoted themselves to a most satisfying routine of prayer, Bible study, singing, and creating a truly Christian community right within the walls of the JC Cathedral.

Oh, it was a glorious time. People treated each other as family, cared for each other when they were sick, shared with each other when they had means, prayed and studied and grew into a loving little community of believers right there on Sixth and Mason.

The Reporter watched this time and once again drew a little church on his notepad. Inside the church, he wrote:

"God's people are really God's family, and it's beautiful when they treat each other as such."

Scene Four:

A Desperate Woman

One day as one of the younger members of the new JC Cathedral opened the front doors to bring in a shipment of groceries, he noticed a woman crying outside the bar across the street. He stared at her for a long time, watching the sobs shake her slumped body as she sat curled up on the pavement. Finally he stepped out of the doorway and crossed the street.

"Miss," he asked awkwardly, "are you all right?"

She looked up at him for a moment, then began sobbing with renewed vigor. Finally she mouthed, "No-o-o."

The young man crouched down next to her. "What's wrong?" he asked.

Trying to regain some semblance of composure, the woman mumbled, "I threw them all way, I did. J-just threw them all away."

"What are you talking about?"

"Last night . . . I been trying to quit, really I have. But last night I just *needed* a drink, you know? It got to where I thought I'd go crazy if I didn't get a drink, just to settle my nerves and relieve some stress, you know?" She started to tear up again. "I was only gonna leave them for an hour. My kids, I mean. I-I never meant to stay out all night. But I guess they got scared when I didn't come back. They called 911. And this morning Social Services came and took them away from me. Said I was an alcoholic and an unfit mother. Oh God, what did I do? What did I do?"

The woman's head drooped into her lap again as silent convulsions rippled through her matted hair and down into her body.

The young man paused, then said, "Listen, I—"

Just then he heard Spire's voice call out in alarm. "Who left this church door open?"

The young man looked up guiltily just in time for Spire to catch his eye. With a firm look on her face, Spire marched across the street and stared him down.

"Get back in the church," she said. "Now."

"Please," it was the crying woman now. "Please, can someone in your church help me?"

Spire surveyed the woman in a glance. *Alcoholic,* she thought. *Probably uses drugs too. No doubt she sleeps around.* She shook her head pityingly and turned to walk back into the church without saying a word. The young man quickly fell in step beside her, leaving the disconsolate young woman weeping on the pavement.

As they entered the safety of the church, Spire scolded the young man. "You're lucky I came along when I did. How do you think our Lord feels seeing you flirting with that kind of trash? You should be ashamed."

And the young man was. He didn't even realize he had been flirting. But if Spire said it, it must be true. He hung his head and went straight to the chapel to pray and repent.

The next morning, Spire had everyone

pack up his or her things. "We're moving," she said. "Before this filthy neighborhood lets Satan dirty us all." One by one Spire's followers silently filed out of the church, never to be seen in that area of the city again.

The Reporter watched as they marched steadily north toward who knows what. This was certainly becoming a confusing assignment. He spread out the next page of his notebook and, as had now become his custom, drew the outline of a church. Inside it he wrote:

He thought for a moment more, then added these words to his drawing:

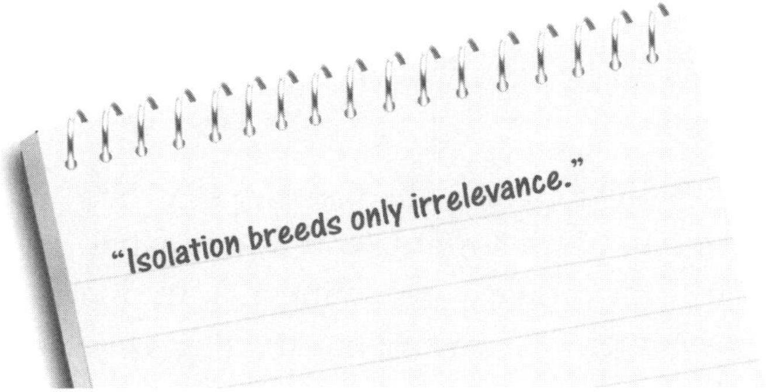

"Isolation breeds only irrelevance."

Just as he finished writing he heard a shout. Cuff's group had finally arrived.

Act Three:
The Major Arrives

Scene One:
Into The Combat Zone

"There it is, straight ahead!" Randall Cuff could barely contain his excitement. "Just like the army of Israel in the days of Moses, we had to wander in the wilderness for a season. But God has given us the victory!"

Cuff clapped his hands and brought the rest of his group to order. Their weariness gave way to delight at the sight of JC Cathedral once more. None of them had expected this search to last for months—but it had. This sprawling city engulfed miles and miles of territory, and with Randall Cuff as the leader, they were determined not to let any stone go unturned. Cuff had told them that no battle was won in just a day, so they had persevered. Finally, after searching the entire southeastern section of Municipa City, they had begun slowly working their way toward downtown—and now that diligence had finally paid off.

Cuff said, "Today we've seen the victory. We've finally found our church home once again."

He turned to survey the church and its new neighborhood. His eyes narrowed a bit at the sight of the arena next door, and at the movie theater on the other side. He spat in disgust when he spotted the lively activity at the bar across the street.

"Friends," he said soberly, "it appears we've only won a single battle, not the war. We have been placed right in the middle of a combat zone between God and the devil." Then his eyes fell on the church once more, and warmth filled his heart at the sight of the strong, impenetrable walls that surrounded it. "Well, by God, we will fight then," he said with determination. "And we will win!"

Cuff clapped his hands again, three short bursts. By now his followers were well trained, and they immediately formed ranks and stood at attention. Cuff turned to the fit young woman at his side and growled, "Take 'em in, Lieutenant."

"Saints, march!" she shouted in response. Then, like the fine Christian soldiers they were, they marched in perfect unison toward the front door of the church.

"Company, sound off!" the lieutenant barked.

"Onward, Christian so-o-o-oldiers, marching as to war, with the cross of Jesus, going on before. Left. Left. Left, right, left."

Deep inside, Cuff smiled. It had taken some work, but by the grace of God he had molded this ragtag bunch of Christians into a crack fighting force for Jesus. Now it was time to take this town for the Lord—or die trying.

The Reporter wasn't quite sure what to write when he saw Cuff's crew go marching into the abandoned JC Cathedral. He thought about it for a moment, then wrote this in his now well-marked notebook:

"When it's time to fight a war, it's best if you know who the enemy is—and who it isn't."

Then, forcing his form into step with the same cadence as Cuff's crew's, he fell into the back of the line and followed the army into the fortress. Joining in song, he sensed something amiss about this group and the way they were singing such lyrics. He would stay alert, with his eyes and ears but especially his heart.

Scene Two:
The Devil's Music

Later that night, Major Cuff and his three brightest lieutenants met in the sanctuary to plan strategies for evangelistic conquest of the neighborhood.

The first thing the major and his lieutenants did was start ripping out the drum set from the preaching platform. "Never did like having these instruments of Satan in our church anyway," Cuff said.

"Oh, I don't know," said one of the

younger lieutenants. "Sometimes I enjoy the sound of them when we sing some of the newer praise songs and . . . "

Silence greeted the assembly as Cuff's face turned the slightest shade of red, and the other two lieutenants coughed and stepped away from the coming confrontation.

Cuff assumed a patronizing stance, "You're young, Lieutenant Case, so I'll forgive your indiscretion this time. But you must understand that drums and bass beats are used in pagan ceremonies to call up demons and, therefore, don't belong in any church that worships the true God. Besides, most of those new praise songs are just compromised, worldly music attempting to justify itself by adding in a few words about God."

The matter settled, Cuff turned back to his work at dismantling the drum set.

"But, what about that piano and organ?" Case wondered aloud. "Here in our country they're used by cults to worship false gods. And even that godless rock 'n roll stuff has piano leads in it. I wonder wh—"

"Enough!" roared the major. He leaned to within an inch of his lieutenant's face. "Listen, Case, you're treading on thin ice now! Everybody knows that the piano and the organ were used during the creation of Christianity's most beloved hymns. To even suggest that these holy instruments have anything at all in common with the pagan, unsanctified drums or electric bass is simply absurd! Got it?"

Lieutenant Case was speechless at first, then simply nodded and returned to the work of tearing out the drum set. A few moments later the job was done, and the four leaders began planning their strategy.

"It's obvious we've got a fight on our hands, Major," said the first lieutenant. "And to make matters worse, I found during reconnaissance this afternoon that the ungodly city politicians have just approved plans for a medical clinic to be built on the vacant lot four doors down on this very street."

"Humph," grumbled the second lieutenant. "They call it a 'medical clinic,' but we all know it really means only one thing: wholesale abortion factory. The murderous scum. They should have been aborted themselves."

The third lieutenant looked grimly at Cuff. "So what's the plan, Major?"

Randall Cuff stood to his full height and tapped on the table. Then he reached down into a barracks bag and plopped a heavy leather book on the table's surface. Opening to Ephesians 6:12-13, he read these words from the Bible:

"For we wrestle not against flesh and blood, but against principalities, against powers, against the rulers of the darkness of this world, against spiritual wickedness in high places. Wherefore take unto you the whole armor of God, that ye may be able to withstand in the evil day, and having done all, to stand."

"Amen, Major," said a lieutenant.

"Praise the Lord," said another.

They understood what the Major wanted them to do, without the necessity of further commentary. And with that scripture fresh in their minds, they dismissed, preparing their hearts for war.

Scene Three: *A "Rowdy" Convert*

The next morning was Sunday, so all the troops gathered for a sermon from Major Cuff.

"Last night," the major intoned, "the leadership team and I met to discuss our current situation. The Lord delivered to my heart a word that I shared with them, and now I'd like to share it with you."

He read again the passage from

Ephesians 6:12-13, then paused to look at his audience.

"Ladies and gentlemen," he roared, "WE ARE AT WAR! This is not just some little neighborhood in some big city. This place where we find ourselves is the enemy's territory! The devil's stomping ground! Those people at that bar across the street are soldiers of Satan whether they know it or not! Those construction workers building that medical clinic are an army of abortionists right here on our street! That so-called entertainment at the arena and movie theater? Propaganda that preaches lies to unwitting souls who venture in there! Our course of action is clear. It's time to FIGHT! To smack the devil right in the mouth! To kick ol' Scratch right in the groin and see how he likes tangling with the army of God for once instead of some weak-willed, lily-livered, non-Christian sap!"

He gazed into the congregation, taking time to look each person in the eye. "So what do you say, then? Are you with me?

Will you join me in this all-out assault on the gates of hell? If we stand together with Christ, we WILL NOT BE DEFEATED!"

A chorus of amens and hallelujahs and preach-it-brothers rang out loud in the echoing hallways of the church. The major knew the time for an altar call when he saw one, so he invited all who would fight to come forward and join him at the pulpit as an outward statement of their inward convictions. All of the major's soldiers rushed the stage, and not an eye was dry in the house.

We're gonna win this war, the major thought to himself. *We're gonna win!*

Over the next few weeks the army of God worked hard to retrofit the church until it would meet military specifications. They punched holes in the brick to create portholes for literature launchers. They cut out a swath of the roof on each side from which to lob propaganda grenades. They worked day and night assembling picket signs and photocopying flyers and drawing up petitions and more.

Finally, on the night of the big concert next door, they were ready.

The first people to arrive for the Rowdy Skankers World Refuge Tour were surprised to find chains on the doors of the auditorium and a group of twenty-five picketers rallying in front of the event center.

"No! No! Hell Must Go!" shouted the picketers, giving added gusto to their cry when they saw the would-be concertgoers start to arrive. "Rowdy Skankers Belong in Toilet Tankers!" they shouted.

Up rose the church's picket signs. "God Hates Rowdy Skankers! Don't Make Him Hate You Too!" said one sign. "Devil's Music for Devil's Ears? Not In My Town!" said another.

Things were going along swimmingly until somebody in the crowd hurled a beer bottle toward the protestors. "Courage, soldiers!" affirmed the major. Then he picked up the broken bottleneck and threw it back into the gathering crowd.

A woman screamed, and a man yelled out a curse. Somebody threw a fist at one of the major's soldiers. A lieutenant raced over and returned the fist with a kick to the groin. "Did you see that, Major?" the exultant lieutenant shouted. "I kicked Satan in the groin just like you preached about in your sermon!"

Cuff's first lieutenant jumped onto a brick outcropping and faced the unruly crowd. "You're all going straight to hell!" she screamed with passion. "Jesus hates you, and so do I!"

A cheer went up from the major's army, which was quickly drowned out by the jeers of the now riled-up crowd. Things were quickly getting out of hand, and could have escalated to serious violence if the police and fire department hadn't shown up just then, doing their best to stop the near riot brewing between the concert fans and the army of God.

A firefighter with a large pair of cutters snipped through the chains on one door, then another, and the crowd rolled inside for the show while the police herded Major Cuff and his soldiers to one side. There they were all eventually handcuffed and taken down to the station house to face charges of disorderly conduct and breaking the fire safety code.

In the wee hours of the morning the soldiers returned to the church, tired but brimming with confidence.

"Total victory," said one soldier.

"Did you see the looks on those cops' faces?" said another.

"They'll think twice before scheduling another satanic rock band in our backyard, won't they, Major?"

As they approached the church doors, they saw a skinny young man standing there, waiting.

"I'll handle this," said Cuff.

"Excuse me," said the young man, "but aren't you the guys who were picketing the concert earlier?"

"Yes, son. What about it?" said the major.

"Did you mean what you said about the Rowdy Skankers being of the devil and stuff?"

"Well, son," the major spoke smugly, "it's common knowledge that the drummer is a, well, a homosexual. God hates that sin worse than any other, you know, except maybe being an abortion doctor. So they're obviously of Satan. And besides, their songs are all that noise and beat and all about sex and drugs and demonic desires. So, yes, they're of the devil."

"Geez," said the young man. "You know what? I'm the guitarist for the Rowdy Skankers, and I just never knew. I mean, yeah, the drummer seemed different, but I never guessed he was, you know, gay or anything. And I thought, you know, that we were singing about love and stuff. I didn't even know we were singing about the devil."

The major smiled and put an arm around the young man. "Son, don't you think it's time you went AWOL from Satan and joined God's army instead?"

Two days later, the guitarist from the Rowdy Skankers announced he was quitting the band because he had "got religion now." A month after that he was arrested for plotting the kidnapping of the new doctor at the medical clinic down the street. To his credit, though, he never ratted on his Christian brothers and sisters. Cuff and his lieutenants got off scot-free.

When the judge asked the guitarist if he had any final words to say before sentencing, the young man's only comment was, "Jesus hates that doctor, and so do I."

In the courtroom gallery the members of JC Cathedral cheered their new brother for his staunch refusal to deny their truth. Well, at least until the bailiff threw them out.

Scene Four:
Retreat!

After that, the army spent most of their time lobbing propaganda grenades with Bible verses on them out through the roof of their church and firing tracts out through their rocket launcher windows. When the projectiles would blow up in lines at the theater or in the parking lot at the bar, wads of flyers and tracts would come sailing out, with Scripture and commands for repentance scrawled all over them. A few people sued the church; others ignored the flyers as trash. But every once in a while, someone would come wandering to the front door of the JC Cathedral to ask questions, and the major himself would handle recruiting and indoctrination, until slowly their numbers swelled to more than a hundred soldiers.

Then, late one night, Major Cuff

gathered his troops in the sanctuary. "Soldiers," he announced, "I've just found out there is a warrant out for my arrest. As the Good Book says somewhere, 'He who fights and runs away, lives to fight another day.' So I've decided it's time for us to move into the next state and take the battle with Satan there. I've found a remote location where we can build a compound. We can set up our own printing press to publish the truth so people will not have to rely on the lies perpetrated by the liberal media. It'll be months before the law can catch up to us, and we'll have delivered another deadly blow to the devil by keeping me free to preach God's uncompromising Word. This mission is not for the weak-kneed or faint of heart. But if you are called to be a real soldier in God's army, stand straight and be ready to march!"

The cheers that greeted the major's ears made his heart smile. He nodded to the first lieutenant.

"All right, troops, let's MOVE!" she shouted. Then, stealing out in the dead of night, the army of the Lord evaded the police—the evil pawns of the devil—and marched away to freedom, leaving the JC Cathedral empty once more.

As they left the Reporter watched with a peculiar feeling. Was it admiration of Major Cuff? After all, here was a man who was dedicated, disciplined, ready to die for his cause. But the Reporter realized it wasn't admiration he felt, but sorrow. Finally, when the last soldier had disappeared into the darkness, he opened his notebook, drew the outline of the church, and inside it wrote words that he remembered were once spoken by the Publisher:

Then he closed his book. He was getting tired. Perhaps now the Publisher would let him go home. He listened intently for the call to come, but only heard silence. When he opened his eyes it

was morning, and there standing in front of the church was Eliara Link.

Act Four: The Remaining Link

Scene One: *A Great Opportunity*

She stood there alone, openmouthed and ecstatic at her discovery. After so long, she had finally found the JC Cathedral! Months ago she had sent the rest of her team home. Well, actually most had already gone home anyway, so she had just sent away the remaining few. But Eliara had never given up a secret hope of finding the Church again.

It had taken her a while, but she finally had come to the conclusion that Nameless had actually been right about Who moved her church. She felt certain now that God Himself had reached down and taken the JC Cathedral out of the comfort zone of its members and replanted it in a place where He wanted it to flourish.

She stepped toward the brick and mortar of the building and wondered why it was so quiet. Had it been sitting in silent disuse this whole time? She examined it more closely and saw signs that someone had been here in the not too distant past. The walls were scarred and, in some places, burned. Graffiti marred the sidewalk and doors. Holes in the sides of the church were chipped and broken as if something had been blasted out through them. She shook her head. This church looked as if it had been in the middle of a war zone.

Cautiously, she opened the front doors

to the church and peeked inside. She smiled. Everything there was just as she had remembered it—the lobby area, the auditorium, Sunday school classrooms, church offices—it was all there. And, in a bit of a surprise, she observed that it was all very well kept. Whatever it was that had attacked the outside of the church had mercifully been kept from destroying its inside.

She peeked out of one of the holes (windows?) in the outer wall and for the first time noticed her surroundings.

"What a marvelous opportunity!" Eliara Link said to herself as she surveyed the scene. "Thank heaven!"

With that she scurried away to call the others. This they had to see.

The Reporter watched Link leave with curiosity and a new sense of hope. Something about that woman was inspiring, but he wasn't sure what it was. Still, since he had gotten quite into the habit by now, he flicked open his notebook and jotted down these words:

> "When Jesus is involved, every obstacle is a potential opportunity."

Then he put down his pen and waited. He didn't have to wait long.

It was just after noon when Eliara Link returned with twenty-three of the twenty-five members of her search party. (The other two members had moved away just last month.) Beaming proudly, she motioned to the JC Cathedral.

"Well," she said. "What do you think?"

When no one responded right away, she continued, "It needs some work, of course, but look at all the ministry opportunities around it." She pointed toward the corner of the street. "See that? I think that person may even be an unwed mother or something. And look, at the bar, there are all kinds of lonely people already. Let alone at the movies or the arena. Isn't it marvelous?"

It didn't take long for Link's enthusiasm to catch on. Soon the other members of her group were chattering away about improvements to make in the building so it would be more accessible to the poor, downtrodden masses. They began making plans for ministry outreach programs and discussing all kinds of other ideas. Over the next few days they all moved into the JC Cathedral and then tore down the front wall of the church so it would be open to the public anytime and all the time.

Afterwards, they held a ministry brainstorming committee meeting in one of the empty Sunday school classrooms to outline their next course of action.

"I noticed yesterday," said one loyal

follower, "that the line at the movie theater was filled with dozens of teenagers from around here. Since we've got them right next door, we ought to plan some kind of outreach to help them with the problems of adolescence, don't you think?"

"Amen, sister," said several others. Link quickly nodded her approval and wrote "Teen Outreach" on the chalkboard.

Another man stood and said, "I stayed out late last night, just watching the streets, and I discovered a group of people out behind the bar across the street." He shook his head sadly. "I couldn't make out everything, but it looked as though they might have been using drugs together—and they were even sharing the same needles."

The group felt immediately sympathetic, and Link wrote on the board "Drug Abuse Prevention."

A couple stood now and began to share. "Eddie and I took a walk around the block this morning and discovered a medical clinic on the corner," said the woman. "There were so many young mothers sitting in the waiting room." The man now spoke up, "They were obviously short on cash. We were thinking maybe we could start some kind of support group for them or something."

Link clapped her hands with excitement and wrote "Ministry to Single Mothers."

"Oh, isn't this exciting?" Eliara Link said to her group. "This is exactly the kind of thing Jesus would do, isn't it? Reaching out to the poor, the sinners, the needy, to share God's love with one's neighbors."

Everyone applauded then, and they all held hands and sang a hymn before heading off to bed. The next morning they hung a new sign out front that said "JC Cathedral: Under New Management" and went quickly to work.

Scene Two: *Taking It to the Streets*

Several group members walked down the corner to the medical clinic and struck up conversations with the young mothers there, intent on getting to know the clientele. The Teen Outreach Committee set about gathering supplies and educational information to share with kids at the movies. And the Drug Abuse Prevention team went to work researching the factors of drug abuse. Within a few short weeks, all three programs were running full throttle.

Eliara Link was so pleased by the tireless work of her team. They were really making a difference in this community where God had placed them. She decided one night to take a look around at the individual ministries.

Link stared at the movie theater where

several volunteers were handing out small packets to the teenagers in line waiting to see *Caterwauling 2: The Return of Scary Sex.*

"Oh, Eliara!" said one volunteer, breaking away from a circle of young people. "So glad you're here! We've been trying so hard to come up with a way to meet teens right where they're living—and we've finally found a way. These new condoms we're passing out are a big hit with the kids! Look!"

She held up a packet and pulled out a few decoratively wrapped condoms for inspection. On the wrappers were printed "God Is Love—1 John 4:8." Inside the bags were flyers explaining correct condom use, statistics on sexually transmitted diseases, and an invitation to attend church services at JC Cathedral on Sunday.

Link smiled her approval. "Wonderful." she said. "We all know most of these kids are going to have sex, and all the sermons in the world are not going to stop that. Now we can rest easy knowing that—

thanks to the ministry of JC Cathedral—those teens who do have sex will be having *safe* sex."

"Excuse me," said a young man shyly stepping out of line with his girlfriend. "Are you the people giving out the free, um, you know, things in the wrappers?" The girl blushed a little and looked away.

Link immediately put them at ease. "Why yes, we are. Would you like a packet? Here, have a packet for you, young man, and one for you too, young lady." She patted the boy on the shoulder and held up a condom. "And remember, God is love!"

Next Link went over to the Drug Abuse Prevention info table her people had set up in front of the church. A small group of people had gathered eagerly around the table.

Look how the Lord is blessing our efforts! she thought to herself. At the table she found Tara giving a short sermon to the gathered people.

"So, you see," Tara said with passion,

"God loves you. Yes, He wants to help you stop taking drugs. But not until you are ready, and that might take years. In the meantime, He doesn't intend for you to catch AIDS or some other disease through an addiction to drugs. That's why we have these for you, just to share a little of God's great love with you."

She tore open a box filled with new, sanitized hypodermic needles.

The people crowded close in to the table where cheerful volunteers from JC Cathedral distributed two or three "clean" needles to each person there. As the crowd was breaking up, Tara called out, "Remember, there's always more where these came from. And don't forget to tell your wives, kids, and friends to attend our support class to help them understand all you are going through right now. It's Friday night in the sanctuary. We hope to have a big crowd."

Link just beamed. There had to be at least two dozen drug users at this little gathering. They really were reaching these people.

Link stepped inside and came upon a member of her team who was counseling a young, obviously pregnant, girl. The counselor was saying, ". . . just like how God works? Praise the Lord!"

Link's curiosity got the best of her. "What's going on in here?" she asked. "What did God do this time?"

The counselor smiled and looked to the girl for approval. Then he said, "Well, Eliara, you know Leah here?" He motioned toward the young mother. "Last week we found out that Leah is pregnant. Again. And, of course, her boyfriend wants nothing to do with a baby. Again. I explained to Leah the complications of raising children in this world without the financial support of the father. Then we prayed that God would bring a solution and, well, He did."

Link could hardly contain herself. "How? What happened?"

"Well, Ms. Link," the young mother said, "I found out that the clinic on the corner will perform an abortion for me for only fifty dollars. But I didn't have fifty dollars . . ."

"But guess what happened just today?" asked the bright-eyed counselor. "Out of the blue I got a check from the IRS for—get this—exactly fifty dollars! They said there'd been an addition error on my tax return, and they were refunding the amount of the error. So obviously I knew God wanted that money to be used to answer our prayers for Leah here. Now she can get that abortion and not have any more worries about bringing an unwanted child into this world."

Link was thrilled. How like God to provide a way where there was no way. She looked at Leah and wondered why the girl could have such sad eyes after getting great news like this. Link gave the girl a hug. "Isn't that wonderful?" she said. "And remember, Leah, Jesus loves you!"

The girl nodded and returned to her seat, one hand involuntarily on her stomach, eyes staring down at the floor.

Link retired that night with a good feeling in her bones. This ministry she had started was really making a difference.

Sunday services were packed. In fact, so many non-Christians were there that Link suggested that the speaker not read from the Bible or make too much out of "the whole Jesus thing."

"We don't want to offend our new guests," she said. The speaker agreed wholeheartedly and spent the time sharing a standard motivational "If-you-can-dream-it-you-can-achieve-it" speech he had given at work several times.

Over the next few months, business boomed at the JC Cathedral. So much so that Link and the others decided to drop "Cathedral" from the name and just call it the "JC House." By doing that, they could then apply for federal grants not available to religious institutions. Of course, then they had to remove any overt connection with Christ in the church, but that was a small price to pay for the ministry that was happening there.

Scene Three:
Time To Move On

Inexplicably, attendance began dropping off. The Ministry to Single Mothers group collapsed when one of the male counselors had an affair with a woman in the group, and Link had yet to find anyone else to take on that job. The owner of the movie theater got an injunction banning the church from handing out any more packets to kids in line, saying it was turning his theater into a "sex hangout instead of an entertainment establishment." The men and women involved in the Drug Abuse Prevention ministry were shaken when two of their number contracted AIDS despite using clean needles, and several others ended up in drug recovery hospitals after inexplicable "bad trips." One longtime user even died. When that happened, those who were left just silently moved on until hardly anyone came to the free needle distributions anymore.

"I don't understand it," Eliara Link said to her leadership team one afternoon. "God was blessing us so much—we had hundreds of people in this church just a few months ago. What happened?"

"Eliara," said one faithful follower, "maybe it's time for us to move again. I mean, God moved us once when He moved our church from the outskirts of the city and placed us here, downtown. Maybe He wants us to move again."

Link thought for a moment, then broke out in a broad smile. "Of course. That's it, isn't it? This was our training ground so we could learn how to effectively minister to hurting people; now God wants us to share those ministry strategies with other churches across the nation! Isn't it wonderful?"

Two weeks later Link and her followers moved out of the JC House and began a teaching ministry to churches across the country, helping them reach out to hurting people just the way she and her team had done in downtown Municipa City.

After they had left, the Reporter took a stroll through the neighborhood. He shook his head. In spite of the entire "ministry" that had gone on in the JC House the past several months, he was hard pressed to find anyone better off because of it. Finally he returned to his post outside the church and opened his notebook once again. Then he wrote:

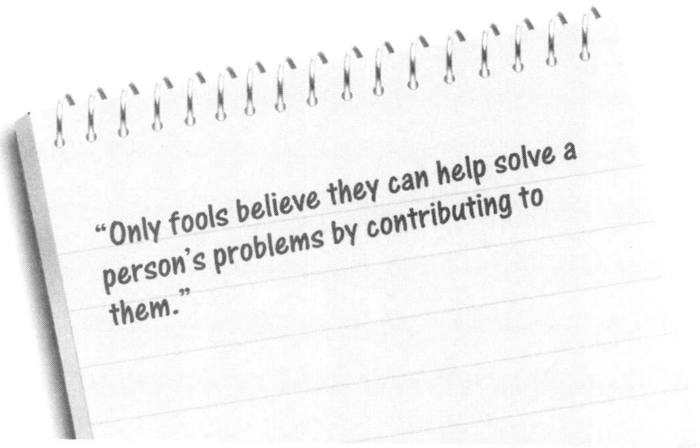

"Only fools believe they can help solve a person's problems by contributing to them."

And after rereading that, he added:

"Good intentions can sometimes be just as harmful as bad ones."

Then the Reporter waited. It was a long wait, but that was okay. He wasn't really enjoying this assignment anyway.

Act Five:
Nameless Picks Up the Pieces

Scene One:
Going Back Home

It was three full years before Nameless found his way to the former JC Cathedral, his search long ago abandoned. By then it was an empty shell of a building. The wall-less front had left the interior exposed to weather and vandalism damage. Now the pews were rotting;

garbage and litter were strewn all over the inside. Water damage had weakened several interior walls. And the smell of decay was downright revolting.

Nameless only thought about the church now because of his work as a clerk in the city's zoning department. For the first few days after the church's disappearance, Nameless had led his group of volunteer searchers throughout the city, but to no avail. The people of Group Four tired quickly of the search, as did others in the town. The local paper had made it a front-page story the first day. Then a few more stories ran, but they were relegated to the religion section. After that, and for most of the next three years, there was little if any discussion of the JC Cathedral in Municipa City. Nameless sometimes thought it had all been a dream.

Then last month, a builder had requested permission to demolish the structure and replace it with a row of small retail businesses. At the last minute, the builder had moved the project to a different location. So Nameless decided perhaps it was time to check out what had happened at the church.

Nameless stood in front of the open wall and stared inside at the filth and debris. *Who had been in here?* he wondered. He had heard rumors that one of the other groups had found the building, but since no one invited Nameless and his group, they had eventually split up and joined a variety of other churches in the city.

Now he looked into this once proud building and simply felt sad. He stood there for a long time—a half-hour, forty-five minutes, an hour—just staring sadly into the mess. While he stood there, a vision began to form in his mind. He shook his head. Naah, it was impossible. But still, the dream wouldn't go away, and finally he returned to work and requested permission from the city to begin restoring the historic JC Cathedral. When permission was granted, Nameless went to work.

Scene Two: *Jake Lends a Hand*

Every Saturday from then on, Nameless spent several hours at the church. Sometimes his wife and children joined him. Sometimes he worked alone. First he replaced the worn and beaten JC House sign with a new one that read, "JC Cathedral—Under Construction." Then he spent weeks simply sweeping out the garbage that had collected there—old condoms, medical supplies, tracts, flyers, obsolete computer equipment, and more. Sometimes he wore a surgical mask to help cover the rotting smell. When he was finally done, all he was left with was the shell of a building. Nothing inside but concrete flooring and interior walls.

Next Nameless began laying bricks to rebuild the front wall. He also made plans for new roofing to fill in the holes that had been cut out of the building. That was when the bartender from across the street finally came over.

"Hey," said the bartender.

"Hello," said Nameless, straightening up to shake the man's hand.

"Listen, I've been watching you for a while, and I finally just had to come over and ask, what are you doing here?"

Nameless smiled. "Well, this was once my home. I'm trying to fix it up again."

"Uh-huh. What about those other Christians who were here before you?"

"What about 'em?" Nameless grinned again and resumed his work.

The bar owner stood for a moment longer, not sure what to do. Then Nameless spoke, "Hey, hand me that brick over there, willya?"

"Sure, sure," said the bartender. "By the way, my name's Jake."

"Nice to meet you, Jake. They call me Nameless."

Jake cocked his head to one side. "No offense, mister, but that's an odd name. Why do you go by that?"

Nameless shrugged and smiled again. "Well, after I became a Christian, I figured my name wasn't what mattered anymore. All that mattered was His Name."

Jake knelt down beside Nameless and began clearing a spot for the next brick. "Interesting," he said. "Can you tell me anything more?"

They worked together the rest of the afternoon, talking, laughing, sweating. When they were done, the bartender shook Nameless's hand and said, "Maybe I'll see you next week then."

"I'd sure appreciate the help."

Over the next several weeks, more of the neighbors came out to chat, encouraged by seeing the bartender with Nameless. Sometimes they talked about Jesus; sometimes they just talked about each other. Soon Jake was bringing his whole family to work on the church on Saturdays, and afterward Jake's family and Nameless's family and anybody else who wanted to join in would head over to a sandwich shop for dinner.

The owner of the arena came along once, and when he heard about Nameless's vision to restore the old church, he decided to get involved. At the next concert (The Dixie Boys Blues Band), he asked Nameless to explain the project to the concert audience during intermission. Afterward, the arena owner raised several thousand dollars from donations by the concert-goers. Nameless used the money for sidewalk improvements required by the city, and since he figured his neighbors would all need the improvements sooner or later too, Nameless paid for their sidewalks to be fixed up as well.

Scene Three:
A Spark of Life

Before long, several people working on the project—including Jake the bartender—had joined Nameless, not just as workers, but as Christians. They began to hold a little Bible study in the basement of the church on Sunday nights.

After a while, Nameless and his new friends decided to set up a small coffee shop/recreation room for teenagers to use before and after their movies next door. They donated the refreshments and also placed several Bibles and some Christian literature in the room for the young people to read and talk about. Soon after, the movie theater owner came over to see why all the kids were leaving his theater in such a hurry to come to the church. He was so impressed that he invited Nameless and Jake to join him for a free sneak preview showing of *Caterwauling 3: More of the Same.*

Nameless smiled, "I'd love to take in a movie with you, but *Caterwauling 3* isn't really my taste. Is there another show anytime soon?"

That was the beginning of a great friendship, and before long the theater owner also had joined Nameless's little Bible study group. Over the many months that followed, news about Nameless and his new friends spread all around the neighborhood.

When a drug addict came looking for help to be free of his addiction, Jake volunteered to go through a rehab program with him, to be moral support and a friend through the process. Halfway through, Jake's rehab partner also came to meet Jesus as a result of Jake's example and story. Similar stories began circulating all around the new JC Cathedral. Nameless's wife started meeting with a group of single mothers, teaching basic parenting skills and becoming a kind of mother figure for them all.

Scene Four:
Healing Hurts

One day a man in a torn and dirty military uniform showed up at the front door of the JC Cathedral.

"Cuff?" said Nameless. "Randall Cuff, is that you?"

The major simply nodded and walked slowly inside. After a cup of hot coffee and a few pleasantries, Cuff told his story.

"We went into the next state," he explained sadly, "and there was mutiny." He sighed. "I spent so much time in my holy war for God that I neglected my family. When my wife divorced me, there was no stemming the flood. The rest of the group said I was now an adulterer and no longer fit to lead them. They booted me off the compound I had built. After all I'd done for them."

Nameless introduced the major to a few of his new friends. At first Cuff was shocked to see people like Jake and the theater owner in the church, and his first instinct was to march them out, but when he found out they were now Christians too, Cuff could only weep.

"I'm sorry," he said after a long moment of silence. "I thought you were my enemy, but instead the enemy made me yours."

Cuff, no longer standing ramrod straight, joined the new Bible study group and soon was on his way to healing. It was he who first noticed Spire on the street. She looked older now, weary, as though she had traveled many, many miles. All she said to Cuff was, "They said I was too worldly, that if I were truly doing God's will I wouldn't need medicine for my heart. That I would never have had that heart attack in the first place." She looked down.

Cuff didn't say anything, but instead led her back into the JC Cathedral where she could find people who would love her, help her, and pray for her recovery—

both physical and emotional.

The group never heard from Link directly, but they heard about her in the news from time to time. She had become a prominent figure in politics of late, running on a social agenda platform that included widespread health and welfare aid for marginalized segments of society. She talked about God quite often, but distanced herself from being known as "Christian"—unless it was a perceived political advantage. Nameless never found out if she had won the election or not, and, to be honest, he didn't much care.

The Bible study group finally grew to the point that it was too large to meet in the church basement, so they started meeting on Sunday mornings in the auditorium instead. When the day finally came for the ribbon-cutting ceremony on the restored church building, many people from the neighborhood gathered to witness the event.

"You finally did it," Jake said to his

good friend, clapping Nameless on the shoulder. "You rebuilt the church."

Nameless just shook his head and smiled. "Naah. I just helped build a building. God rebuilt the church."

He looked at the people standing around him, smiling, hurting people all gathered to celebrate only one Name—His Name.

"After all," Nameless said, "the real Church isn't a building at all; it's the presence of Christ within the hearts and lives of people. Our obligation then is just to share that Presence with our world."

Epilogue: The Reporter's Notebook

The Reporter's broad face brightened just then, as he watched Nameless and Jake and the others move inside for a worship service. Then he heard it—the call had finally come. It was time to shed this cramping disguise and go home. Another had been assigned to take over the Reporter's task from here on out.

Stiffly at first, Reporter flexed his wings and reveled in the feeling of freedom that movement brought. Then, with little more than a thought, he melted away the tie, the shirt, the camera, the tape recorder, and everything else he had burdened himself with these many months. The only thing he kept was his trusty little notebook. Before returning to his Publisher, he took one last look through the pages of his book. Here is what he read:

"When the church is missing, you'd better go out and find it."

"Does God need to be protected and walled off from those in His world?"

"God's people are really God's family, and it's beautiful when they treat each other as such."

"The Christian who will not touch his or her culture can never change it."

"Isolation breeds only irrelevance."

"When it's time to fight a war, it's best if you know who the enemy is—and who it isn't."

"God did not send His Son to condemn the world, but to save it."

"When Jesus is involved, every obstacle is a potential opportunity."

"Only fools believe they can help solve a person's problems by contributing to them."

"Good intentions can sometimes be just as harmful as bad ones."

Then the Reporter decided to add two last observations to his notebook:

"In the end, all that matters is Jesus."

"The real Church isn't a building at all; it's the Presence of Christ within the hearts and lives of Christian people. Our obligation then is just to share that Presence with our world."

Satisfied, the Reporter looked longingly toward heaven.

And then he was gone.

Discussing "Who Moved My Church?"

The workshop leader finished his story and waited. Several people in the group were nodding their heads; more than a few wore puzzled expressions; one or two looked downright angry.

Gospel Diva spoke first. "To be honest, I don't know quite what to make of this story," she said. "I just know it makes me feel uncomfortable."

Sketcher looked up. "Yeah, me too," he said. Then he shrugged. "But at this point in my life, I think feeling uncomfortable might be a good thing."

Loud Man #2 raised his hand. "So what happens next?" he asked. "Where do we go from here? I need answers, not just a story."

The seminar leader stood and began handing out photocopied sheets of paper. "Use the discussion questions below to explore more deeply the themes of this story," he said. "You can explore them individually or as a group."

The loud men quickly huddled in a circle and began talking in whispers. Gospel Diva, Sketcher, and a few others also joined together to talk over their impressions of the story. Several chose to meditate on the sheet of paper by themselves.

The leader waited until everyone was engrossed in the discussion questions, then he smiled. Quietly he packed up his briefcase and walked out the door. No one noticed for some time that he had gone. But that was okay. There were more pressing matters at hand . . .

• • •

The Seminar Leader's Discussion Sheet for "Who Moved My Church?"

1. What is your initial reaction to the allegory of "Who Moved My Church?"

   Why do you feel that way?

2. Have you seen real life examples of Spire? Cuff? Link? Nameless?

3. Which of the four main characters—Spire, Cuff, Link, or Nameless—most resembles you? Why? Which is the type of person you most like to associate with at church? Why?

4. What positive traits do you find in each of the characters? What weaknesses or flaws do you see in each of them?

5. The story seems to have deliberately left out distinctions like race,

denominational affiliation, and societal status for the main characters. Why do you suppose that is?

6. All of the characters in this allegory truly believed they were interacting with their new culture in ways that God wanted them to—yet they each approached their culture with different goals. Have you seen that kind of thing happen in real life? Why do you suppose it happens? What do you think should be done about it, if anything?

7. What sort of notes do you think the Reporter is making in his notebook about the way you interact with your culture?

8. If you were to summarize the primary message of this story into one sentence, what would you say? Why?

9. What do you think is the most

desirable way for a Christian to interact with his or her constantly changing culture? What keeps you from doing that?

10. How do the following verses apply to this story?

    Acts chapter 10

    Ephesians 6:12-18

    John 17:14,15

    1 John 2:15

Afterword: A Note from the Author

Dear Friend,

First, I would like to thank you for having taken the time to read this little allegory of faith and culture. I know your time is precious, and I don't take it lightly that you have spent it on this book.

I also realize that by now it is very possible that something in this book has made you angry with me. Fact is, rereading this allegory got me a little steamed at myself as well.

You see, I would like to say that every character I wrote about in this book is someone I have met or someone I know. But that would be only part of the truth.

The whole truth is that every character in this book is really one I have seen in myself over the past two decades since I became a follower of Christ. Oh, not all at once, mind you. But yesterday I have to admit something of Major Cuff came out in my life. And before that the socially susceptible attitude of Eliara Link made an appearance as well. And today? Well, today I just want to isolate myself like the good Althea Spire and ignore the fact that people are in desperate need all around me.

Yet, by the saving grace of God, there are times when Nameless does pop up in my life too. Rare times, to be honest. But his devotion to his Lord and his desire to touch his culture with the healing hand of Christ does come out from time to time.

So what does that mean? That I am perfect and you are not? Absurd. That you and I are right and the rest of the body of Christ is hopelessly making a mess of things? No, not that either.

It means that Christ Himself has moved His Church and planted it directly into the volatile, ever changing culture of America in the twenty-first century. Now you and I must decide how we will let our faith in Jesus touch the people around us, how we will let the fingers of God move us as we live in this world, but not of it.

When He walked the earth, Jesus was totally immersed in the culture of His time—so much so that He often used cultural references to bring home the truth of God. And yet He also managed to remain completely apart from the sinfulness of that culture and keep Himself unstained by wrongdoing. How could He move so easily from a party with "sinners" to the pulpit of a local synagogue—and remain totally holy and totally loving at the same time?

I wish I had all the answers for us on that topic, but I don't. In the end, with this little allegory I guess I am asking questions more than I am providing answers. If so, then, like the leader of the seminar in Denver, I have accomplished my objective, which is to "help us think through what it means to be Christians in our culture today."

But I do know this. If indeed there is an angel of God observing my progress as a part of the universal Church of Jesus, I know what I want his report to say about me.

"In just the right light, he looks something like the Publisher."

I hope that is what you want too. Meanwhile, let's make a promise to each other, shall we? Let's determine to join together to be the true body of Christ to our culture today—no matter where God may choose to move His Church tomorrow.

Thanks for your attention.

Sincerely yours,
Mike Nappa

About the Author

Mike Nappa is the author and coauthor of dozens of books, many of which are bestsellers. At present there are more than a million copies of his books in print. He is also a former youth pastor; the founder of Nappaland.com, "The Free Webzine for Families"; founding president of the Christian media company Nappaland Communications Inc.; and the popular radio personality/ cultural commentator featured in *MovieSpot Live,* which airs weekly on KPXQ radio station in the Phoenix metropolitan area.

In addition to his books, Mike has written more than four hundred magazine and Internet articles for numerous publications such as *Group, Junior High Ministry, ParentLife, Living with Teenagers, HomeLife, Christian Single, FaithWorks, Campus Life, Breakaway, Brio, On Course, Focus on the Family Clubhouse,* Crosswalk.com, CBN.com, Christianity.com, Nappaland.com, and many others. Mike and his work have also been featured in many high-profile television, radio, and print media outlets such as *The 700 Club, First Edition, Decision Today, Marriage Partnership, CBA Marketplace, Christian Retailing, Publisher's Weekly,* and more.

Mike can be contacted through his web site at www.Nappaland.com.

Additional copies of this book and other titles by RiverOak Publishing are available from your local bookstore.

If you have enjoyed this book, or if it has impacted your life, we would like to hear from you.

Please contact us at:

RiverOak Publishing
Department E
P.O. Box 700145
Tulsa, Oklahoma 74170-0145

Or by e-mail at:
info@riveroakpublishing.com

Visit our website at:
www.riveroakpublishing.com